POETRY SAFARI 2023

Wildest Dreams

Edited By Andy Porter

First published in Great Britain in 2023 by:

YoungWriters®
Est. 1991

Young Writers
Remus House
Coltsfoot Drive
Peterborough
PE2 9BF
Telephone: 01733 890066
Website: www.youngwriters.co.uk

All Rights Reserved
Book Design by Ashley Janson
© Copyright Contributors 2023
Softback ISBN 978-1-80459-803-0

Printed and bound in the UK by BookPrintingUK
Website: www.bookprintinguk.com
YB0558L

FOREWORD

Dear Reader,

Welcome to this book packed full of feathery, furry and scaly friends!

Young Writers' Poetry Safari competition was specifically designed for 4-7 year-olds as a fun introduction to poetry and as a way to think about the world of animals. They could write about pets, exotic animals, dinosaurs or even make up their own crazy creature! From this starting point, the poems could be as simple or as elaborate as the writer wanted, using imagination and descriptive language.

Given the young age of the entrants, we have tried to include as many poems as possible. Here at Young Writers we believe that seeing their work in print will inspire a love of reading and writing and give these young poets the confidence to develop their skills in the future. Poetry is a wonderful way to introduce young children to the idea of rhyme and rhythm and helps learning and development of communication, language and literacy skills.

These young poets have used their creative writing abilities, sentence structure skills, thoughtful vocabulary and most importantly, their imaginations, to make their poems and the animals within them come alive. I hope you enjoy reading them as much as we have.

CONTENTS

Abingdon Preparatory School, Frilford

Paksun Sze (7)	1
Haolin Wang (6)	2
William Morley (7)	3
Dylan Ge (7)	4
Jacob Midwinter (7)	5
Benjamin Ruang-Oun	6
Rex Rice (7)	7
Charlie Francis (7)	8
Alois Bhatia (7)	9

Amberley Parochial School, Amberley

Harrison Seymour (7)	10
Ellie Searle-Edwards (7)	11
Molly Hunnisett-Bees (7)	12
Jessie Searle-Edwards (7)	13
Max Elmer (6)	14
Bonnie Gilroy (7)	15
Isla Henderson (5)	16
Georgia du Rose (6)	17
Jake Webster (7)	18
Daniel Smith (6)	19
Sylvester Bendixson (7)	20
Mia Westmore (6)	21
Bertie D	22
Gilbert Brownlee-Williams (6)	23

Cuddington Croft Primary School, Cheam

Sienna Clements (5)	24
Izzy Wood (5)	25
Aishvi Chunduru (5)	26
Evelyn Yuen (5)	27
Owsley Ford-Aldred (5)	28
Imogen (5)	29
Ava Silva-Gill (5)	30
Kasper Li (5)	31
Enoch Ahabwe (5)	32
Malia Jyothish (5)	33
Cassander Butler-White (5)	34
Matthew King (5)	35
Sholan Ilanco (5)	36
Sebastian Varrier (5)	37
Henry Rogers (5)	38
James Chan (5)	39
Maxwell Hannah (5)	40
Halle Cooper (5)	41
Lukas Gruzinov (5)	42
Zoey Zuo (5)	43
Justin Spears (5)	44
Rosanna Banfield (5)	45
Martha Godwin (5)	46
Aveen Brar (5)	47
Arin Eames (5)	48
Tommy Dougal (5)	49
Skye Davidson-King (5)	50
Finty Collins (5)	51
Jaxon Neil (5)	52
Evie Vyse (4)	53
Amber Robertson (5)	54
Tom Hassall (5)	55
Iliya Zadehkochak (5)	56

James Pham (5)	57
Aaron Singh (4)	58
Rosie Hawes (4)	59
Jack Field (4)	60
Taye Hameed (5)	61
Harvey Pearce-Costello (5)	62
Nicholas Cox (5)	63
Margot Worsley (4)	64
Ezekiel Graham (5)	65
Karikaalan Matheesan (5)	66
Heidi Brown (5)	67
Lily Powell (5)	68
Oliver Rahnama (4)	69
Harry Bui (5)	70
Jude Murad (5)	71
Cassie Gardner (5)	72

Fairchildes Primary School, New Addington

Melatiah Peeler (7)	73
Arooj Sohail Chaudhary (7)	74
Julia Gorka (6)	75
Soliana Bekele (7)	76
Farren Pickering (7)	77
Levi Amoah (8)	78
Leo Lambeth (6)	79
Blen Berhe (7)	80
Jeremiah Amoah (7)	81
Marios Jones (7)	82
Liliana Cerullo (6)	83
Mia Baraniak (7)	84
Mercedes Adesanya	85
Josiah Amoah (7)	86
Faye Ogbuehi (6)	87
Leo Frost (7)	88

Hadrian Primary School, South Shields

Ariah Blue Griffiths-Proc (5)	89
Emily Scott (5)	90
Josie Willow Johnson (5)	92
Eva Hussain (5)	93

Arthur Deans Coffield (4)	94
Lily-Rose Gonzalez (5)	95
Rosa Mary (4)	96
Adam Elmenshawy	97
Rosie Cain (5)	98

Lawns Park Primary School, Leeds

Rupert Crossdale (6)	99
Sophie Longley (6)	100
Cecelia Manning (6)	101
Amber Ghatrora (5)	102
Elisha Hewson (6)	103

Longshaw Infant School, Blackburn

Jenson Ainsworth (6)	104
Lottie-Mae Egan (5)	105
Olivia Clarke (6)	106
Caleb Bennett (5)	107
Habiba Zanid (6)	108
Skylar Greenwood (6)	109
Sydney Greenwood (6)	110
Draigh Gibbons (6)	111
Alice Lianne Kenny (6)	112
Aurora-Rose Bentley (6)	113
Azma Anwar (6)	114
Letty Riley (5)	115
Winter Daye (6)	116
Baboucarr MP Van Eyndhoven (6)	117
Alexis Williams (6)	118
Jonathan Zagara (5)	119
Bilal Majid (5)	120
Lisa Lin (6)	121
Ionie Clarke (6)	122
Khadija Hafeji (6)	123
Siena Riley (5)	124
Reece Thompson (6)	125
Eva Slater (6)	126
Luke McCardle (6)	127
Lydia Eddleston (5)	128

Isabelle Hargreaves (6)	129
Esmé Newton (6)	130
Riley Ferrari (6)	131
Jack Harris (5)	132
Daisy Wickham (5)	133
Ellis Shaw (5)	134
Nicolle Ndlovu (6)	135
Lily Greenhough (6)	136
Austen Snape (6)	137
Tiffany Abram (6)	138
Alyssa Fitzpatrick (6)	139
Issac Cocker (6)	140
Scarlett Jackson (5)	141
Abigail Zalewska (5)	142
Alfie-James McGlinn (5)	143
Hunter Jackson (6)	144
Seth Nyarambi (6)	145
Aibhlinn Griffiths (6)	146
Eli Martindale (5)	147
Luca Popa (5)	148
Sophia-Lillie Cantwell (5)	149
Caoimhe Hamill (5)	150
Aubrey Hosker (5)	151
Shay Ruddy (6)	152
Maira Bisharet (6)	153

St John's CofE Primary School, Stapleford

Amelia-Rose Lings (7)	154
Lydia Mathison (7)	155
Hanna Bella Herczeg (7)	156
Merry Lyons (7)	157
Clover (7)	158
Zuriella (7)	159
Beth Tan (5)	160
Ronnie Kirkpatrick (7)	161
Abraham Burton (6)	162
Jessica Mann (6)	163
Nico O'Connor (7)	164
Liliya White (6)	165
Callum Allaway (6)	166
Cyrus Bennett (6)	167
Harry McLaughlin (5)	168

Ben White (6)	169
Hollie Hutchinson (6)	170
George (5), Frankie, Harry, Shelby & Hollie (6)	171
Shelby Dackiw (6)	172
Coleson-Christopher Lings (6)	173
Anaya Gajendran (6)	174

St Maria Goretti Primary School, Cranhill

Ella Uzor (7)	175
Aveen Mussa (7)	176
Umar Eskiev (7)	177
Cooper Muir (7)	178
Osewe Inyinbor (7)	179
Isla Clark (7)	180
Orlaith Walsh (7)	181
Ray Campbell (7)	182

St Mary's Primary School, Bellanaleck

Aoife Maguire (7)	183
Aoife McArdle (7)	184
Ella McCusker (7)	185
Sianna McGahey (7)	186
Aibreán Rooney (7)	187
Maria Kelly (7)	188
Kíla Gallagher (7)	189
Charlie Bannon (7)	190
Anna Kelly (7)	191
Shane Maguire-Reilly (7)	192

The Poems

The Grizzly Bear

A grizzly bear has a brown, circular tail.
He scratches his back against a tree.
Leaping to catch his salmon in groups.
Grizzly bears love swimming in sparkly water.
A grizzly bear feels fluffy and cute.
Bears have the best sense of smell.
Is that a growl I can hear?

Paksun Sze (7)
Abingdon Preparatory School, Frilford

The Chameleon

The chameleon feels like a tough, turquoise sphere.
The chameleon tastes like a crunchy leaf.
The chameleon hears a hungry predator approaching its area.
The chameleon looks like a green, lush, curled-up ball.
The chameleon smells like a fresh, four-legged circle.

Haolin Wang (6)
Abingdon Preparatory School, Frilford

The Komodo Dragon

The Komodo dragon is as wrinkly as hands after a bath
It smells using its enormously long tongue
Touches the sand with its razor-sharp teeth
It sees its fast, tasty prey
And tastes the fresh meat of its yummy lunch
Watch out for the Komodo dragon!

William Morley (7)
Abingdon Preparatory School, Frilford

Draco Lizard

The Draco lizard can see lots of yummy bugs crawling on trees,
Feeling rough tree bark beneath its claws,
Tasting crunchy bug shells,
It smells the green, luscious forest, growing around it,
Hearing birds chirping and leaves rustling.

Dylan Ge (7)
Abingdon Preparatory School, Frilford

Python

The python feels scaly like a coat.
The python looks around the lush, green jungle.
The python looks like a long, scaly handbag.
The python hears the trees swish in the forest.
The python tastes like a scaly pile of raw meat.

Jacob Midwinter (7)
Abingdon Preparatory School, Frilford

Benjamin

The fluffy panda feels like a fluffy cat.
The panda tastes bamboo.
The panda hears waterfalls, falling like rain.
The panda sees the trees swishing from left to right.
The panda smells the soft wind and the breeze.

Benjamin Ruang-Oun
Abingdon Preparatory School, Frilford

The Jaguar

It looks like a yellow and fluffy cat,
And eats an angry brown deer,
It smells the prey,
It feels like smooth, silky fur,
It sounds like nothing.

Rex Rice (7)
Abingdon Preparatory School, Frilford

The Giraffe

See the yellow animal with a very long neck
Hear the munching of crunchy leaves
Smell the forest around
Taste the fresh air
Feel its bumpy skin.

Charlie Francis (7)
Abingdon Preparatory School, Frilford

The Tiger

See the stripy tiger,
Feel his fluffy face,
Smell the fresh new air,
Taste the tiger's prey,
Hear the scratch of the claws.

Alois Bhatia (7)
Abingdon Preparatory School, Frilford

Cat, Ant And Bees

C an be very furry.
A s fun as playing with a friend.
T o love it you must take care of it.

A very strong animal.
N ot very big.
T oo small to see.

B ees making honey.
E ggs being made by the queen.
E ating whatever they eat.
S uch yummy honey.

Harrison Seymour (7)
Amberley Parochial School, Amberley

Starfish

S haped like a star.
T akes food outside its body.
A lways forgets things like me or you.
R eally forgetful.
F ish swim by when it shines bright.
I n the ocean that's where they live.
S wim and see, it's the shiniest thing in the bright blue sea.
H e has no brains.

Ellie Searle-Edwards (7)
Amberley Parochial School, Amberley

Spider

S piders in your attic.
P rickling you everywhere with their little legs.
I n your bed at night, crawling around.
D ead spiders in your hair and in the attic.
E nd of the world for you, the spiders rule!
R unning with their hairy legs.

Molly Hunnisett-Bees (7)
Amberley Parochial School, Amberley

Butterfly

B eautiful creatures
U p in the sky
T ricky to catch
T aking nectar
E legant and pretty
R are
F lies as light as a fairy
L ies with its wings to the sun
Y ou can sometimes see them in the garden.

Jessie Searle-Edwards (7)
Amberley Parochial School, Amberley

Penguin

P inging everywhere
E very member of the pod likes fish
N ever gets lost
G iving up is not an option
U ndefeatable, only an orca can defeat it
I n the water, so graceful
N ever giving up in the water.

Max Elmer (6)
Amberley Parochial School, Amberley

Mouse

M iniature little things.
O h, a mouse went running to its house.
U nder the fridge it goes exploring like a girl and boy.
S mooth on the floor, not like an elephant.
E very sound is as quiet as the floor.

Bonnie Gilroy (7)
Amberley Parochial School, Amberley

Isla

C ows are mums to them.
A s they are little they need some milk.
L ittle cute things leaping around on the cow's common.
F all down a hole, get back up and then find their mum to drink milk.

Isla Henderson (5)
Amberley Parochial School, Amberley

Koala

K ing, cuddling animal.
O n brown eucalyptus leaves.
A beautiful grey animal.
L oving and cute.
A n animal you'd love to see.

Georgia du Rose (6)
Amberley Parochial School, Amberley

Dog And Lion

D irty dog
O bedient and loyal
G lorious.

L azy lion
I t keeps its eyes
O n its prey
N asty beast.

Jake Webster (7)
Amberley Parochial School, Amberley

Sharks

S cary as a snake.
H ungry shark.
A ttacking little fish.
R acing shark.
K illing shark.
S wimming sharks.

Daniel Smith (6)
Amberley Parochial School, Amberley

Sloth

S low and sleepy.
L ying in a tree.
O pening its mouth to let out a yawn.
T ree lover.
H oping for another nap.

Sylvester Bendixson (7)
Amberley Parochial School, Amberley

Cow

C ute, little cow on the common.
O n the common where there are lots of cows.
W hile the cows keep eating the grass.

Mia Westmore (6)
Amberley Parochial School, Amberley

Dog

D igging dogs catch a bone in the garden.
O range dogs run in the house.
G inger dogs fight with cats.

Bertie D
Amberley Parochial School, Amberley

Cat

C ats can climb.
A lways out at night.
T easing their prey.

Gilbert Brownlee-Williams (6)
Amberley Parochial School, Amberley

My Cat Dragon

My cat dragon sounds fierce because it roars
My cat dragon looks amazing because it flies around in circles
My cat dragon feels soft
My cat dragon smells fiery
My cat dragon tastes like fur because it is furry
It is grey and stripy because it is dangerous to touch.

Sienna Clements (5)
Cuddington Croft Primary School, Cheam

Giraffes

Giraffes are tall
Giraffes are cute
Giraffes taste like crisps
Giraffes smell like trash
Giraffes feel soft
Giraffes are patterned
Giraffes sound like, *"Urr urr!"*

Izzy Wood (5)
Cuddington Croft Primary School, Cheam

Pigs

Pigs are nice.
Pigs are hungry.
Pigs taste like vegetarians!
Pigs smell like chocolate.
Pigs are muddy.
Pigs feel squishy.
Pigs sound like, "*Oink oink!*"

Aishvi Chunduru (5)
Cuddington Croft Primary School, Cheam

Unicorns

Unicorns feel smooth
Unicorns smell magical
Unicorns taste like candy
Unicorns sound like, "Mehhh."
Unicorns look wonderful
And rainbowy and colourful with long hair!

Evelyn Yuen (5)
Cuddington Croft Primary School, Cheam

Chameleon

Chameleon smells like a flamingo
Chameleon's tummy is soft
Their head is bumpy
Their tail is fluffy
And the rest of it is tough
Chameleon makes all of the animal sounds!

Owsley Ford-Aldred (5)
Cuddington Croft Primary School, Cheam

Butterflies

Butterflies are colourful
Butterflies are lovely
Butterflies feel ticklish
Butterflies are stripy
Butterflies taste like curls
Butterflies sound like the wind.

Imogen (5)
Cuddington Croft Primary School, Cheam

Unicorns

Unicorns feel like flowers
Unicorns smell like rainbows
Unicorns look shiny, colourful and pretty
Unicorns taste like sweets
Unicorns sound like, "*Hahaha!*"

Ava Silva-Gill (5)
Cuddington Croft Primary School, Cheam

Dinosaurs

Dinosaurs are kind
Dinosaurs smell of meat
Dinosaurs are fluffy
Dinosaurs taste of grass
Dinosaurs sound like, "*Roar!*"
Thump, thump, thump!

Kasper Li (5)
Cuddington Croft Primary School, Cheam

Tigers

Tigers are big
Tigers smell of meat
Tigers are orange and black
Tigers go, "Umnum!"
Tigers feel soft
Tigers nap
Tigers go, "*Rar!*"

Enoch Ahabwe (5)
Cuddington Croft Primary School, Cheam

Monkeys

Monkeys are soft
Monkeys are rainbowy
Monkeys smell of banana
Monkeys are big
Monkeys taste of water
Monkeys sound like, "*Oo, aa!*"

Malia Jyothish (5)
Cuddington Croft Primary School, Cheam

Leopard

Leopard is big
Leopard is spotty
Leopard is fluffy
Leopard smells like grass
Leopard tastes like poo
Leopard goes, "*Rar!*"

Cassander Butler-White (5)
Cuddington Croft Primary School, Cheam

T-Rex

T-rex has sharp teeth
T-rex is scaly
T-rex tastes of yummy
T-rex smells of beef
T-rex feels like a dragon
T-rex sounds like a vulture.

Matthew King (5)
Cuddington Croft Primary School, Cheam

Lions

Lions are strong
Lions are yellow
Lions smell of bunnies
Lions taste of meat
Lions feel fluffy
Lions go, "*Rar!*"

Sholan Ilanco (5)
Cuddington Croft Primary School, Cheam

Cheetahs

Cheetahs have sharp claws
Cheetahs smell like meat
Cheetahs taste like toilets
Cheetahs feel soft
Cheetahs sound like a tiger!

Sebastian Varrier (5)
Cuddington Croft Primary School, Cheam

Tigers

Tigers are fierce
Tigers feel soft and are beautiful
Tigers smell of meat
Tigers can see better than people
Tigers sound loud!

Henry Rogers (5)
Cuddington Croft Primary School, Cheam

Dragons

Dragons sound fierce
Dragons taste like crocodiles
Dragons feel armoured
Dragons smell like ice
Dragons are long and fiery.

James Chan (5)
Cuddington Croft Primary School, Cheam

Pandas

Pandas feel big and soft
Pandas are sleepy
Pandas smell like ice and snow
Pandas taste like fluff
Pandas sound like quiet.

Maxwell Hannah (5)
Cuddington Croft Primary School, Cheam

Giraffe

Giraffe is spotty.
Giraffe feels fluffy.
Giraffe is tasty like me.
Giraffe makes a noise, "*Ning nong!*"

Halle Cooper (5)
Cuddington Croft Primary School, Cheam

Pandas

Pandas feel soft
Pandas are big and sleepy
Pandas smell like fluff
Pandas taste wet
Pandas sound like a soft roar.

Lukas Gruzinov (5)
Cuddington Croft Primary School, Cheam

Elephant

Elephant is big, Elephant is grey
Elephant smells like grass
Elephant feels smooth
Elephant is tasty, Elephant is loud.

Zoey Zuo (5)
Cuddington Croft Primary School, Cheam

My Pig

My pig has a snout for smelling.
I can see a small tail.
My pig has soft, soft skin.
My pig likes to eat cornflakes.

Justin Spears (5)
Cuddington Croft Primary School, Cheam

Dogs

Dogs are fluffy
Dogs are small
Dogs smell of fur
Dogs taste fluffy
Dogs sound like, "*Ruff!*"

Rosanna Banfield (5)
Cuddington Croft Primary School, Cheam

My Lion

My lion is really fluffy.
I can see a long tail on his bottom.
My lion has hairy feet.
My lion likes to eat grass.

Martha Godwin (5)
Cuddington Croft Primary School, Cheam

Cows

Cows are big
Cows are strong
Cows smell of grass
Cows feel cuddly
Cows sound like, "*Moo!*"

Aveen Brar (5)
Cuddington Croft Primary School, Cheam

My Lion

My lion is blue and yellow.
I can see spikes on his face.
I can hear a loud roar.
My lion likes to eat treats.

Arin Eames (5)
Cuddington Croft Primary School, Cheam

My Koala

My koala is grey and fluffy.
I can see a cute koala.
I can feel his soft fur.
My koala eats leaves and socks.

Tommy Dougal (5)
Cuddington Croft Primary School, Cheam

My Giraffe

My giraffe is tall.
I can see her strong muscles.
I can feel her soft fur.
My giraffe likes to eat leaves.

Skye Davidson-King (5)
Cuddington Croft Primary School, Cheam

My Lion

My lion is yellow,
She is fluffy,
She is small,
My lion eats green leaves,
My lion likes to roar.

Finty Collins (5)
Cuddington Croft Primary School, Cheam

My Koala

My koala is furry.
He has glasses to see better.
He has grey soft fur.
My koala likes to eat leaves.

Jaxon Neil (5)
Cuddington Croft Primary School, Cheam

My Lion

My lion is hairy.
I can feel her soft fur.
I can hear her loud roar.
My lion eats leaves and socks.

Evie Vyse (4)
Cuddington Croft Primary School, Cheam

My Giraffe

My giraffe is fluffy.
I can see her pretty face.
She has soft fur.
My giraffe eats green leaves.

Amber Robertson (5)
Cuddington Croft Primary School, Cheam

Lions

Lions are hungry
Lions taste of hair
Lions are fluffy
Lions smell of meat
Lions roar!

Tom Hassall (5)
Cuddington Croft Primary School, Cheam

My Giraffe

My giraffe is big.
He is spotty.
My giraffe has a long neck.
My giraffe eats Shreddies.

Iliya Zadehkochak (5)
Cuddington Croft Primary School, Cheam

My Elephant

My elephant is big.
He is grey.
I can see a long, long trunk.
My elephant eats pants.

James Pham (5)
Cuddington Croft Primary School, Cheam

My Giraffe

My giraffe is tall.
He is yellow.
I can see spots on his body.
My giraffe eats pants.

Aaron Singh (4)
Cuddington Croft Primary School, Cheam

My Koala

My koala is small.
She has such soft fur.
She lives in the jungle.
My koala eats mud.

Rosie Hawes (4)
Cuddington Croft Primary School, Cheam

My Elephant

My elephant is big.
My elephant is soft.
He has a long trunk.
My elephant eats socks.

Jack Field (4)
Cuddington Croft Primary School, Cheam

My Elephant

My elephant is big.
He is soft.
My elephant has blue skin.
My elephant eats people.

Taye Hameed (5)
Cuddington Croft Primary School, Cheam

My Cheetah

My cheetah is fast.
My cheetah is big.
My cheetah has spots.
My cheetah eats meat.

Harvey Pearce-Costello (5)
Cuddington Croft Primary School, Cheam

My Zebra

My zebra is stripy
He is big and round
He lives in the jungle
My zebra eats grass.

Nicholas Cox (5)
Cuddington Croft Primary School, Cheam

My Flamingo

My flamingo is pink.
She is small.
I can see her spots.
My flamingo eats pants.

Margot Worsley (4)
Cuddington Croft Primary School, Cheam

My Tiger

My tiger is big.
My tiger is soft.
My tiger is black.
My tiger lives in a cave.

Ezekiel Graham (5)
Cuddington Croft Primary School, Cheam

My Panda

My panda is big.
My panda is red.
He is fluffy and furry.
My panda eats pants.

Karikaalan Matheesan (5)
Cuddington Croft Primary School, Cheam

My Giraffe

My giraffe is tall.
She is spotty.
She is yellow.
My giraffe eats people.

Heidi Brown (5)
Cuddington Croft Primary School, Cheam

My Elephant

My elephant is pink.
She is pretty.
She is big.
My elephant eats leaves.

Lily Powell (5)
Cuddington Croft Primary School, Cheam

My Monkey

My monkey eats plants
My monkey is big
My monkey lives in the trees.

Oliver Rahnama (4)
Cuddington Croft Primary School, Cheam

My Elephant

My elephant is big.
He has a long nose.
My elephant eats leaves.

Harry Bui (5)
Cuddington Croft Primary School, Cheam

My Giraffe

My giraffe is big
My giraffe is yellow
My giraffe eats birds.

Jude Murad (5)
Cuddington Croft Primary School, Cheam

My Elephant

My elephant is small.
He has a trunk.
My elephant eats bugs.

Cassie Gardner (5)
Cuddington Croft Primary School, Cheam

I Dreamt Of A Unicorn

Last night after saying my bedtime prayer
I dreamt of my sparkly unicorn.
They were galloping with their shadows
Through the hallway leading to my bedroom
Eating my colourful hair beads.
Against my wall they lay on me
Casting spells on my big brother
As they raced about his bed
Spreading rainbows and glitter all around.
They were on my scooter, sofa and stairs.
They were eating all my snacks
As they pranced about the carpet.
There were unicorns, unicorns, unicorns
As far as I could count and see.
Waking up this morning
I noticed glitter all over me and my bed.

Melatiah Peeler (7)
Fairchildes Primary School, New Addington

Poetry Safari

One little monkey, swinging wild and free
Saw five bananas hanging from a tree.
Oh! That monkey, full from lunch
Ate one banana from the bunch.
Oh! That monkey, greedy was he
Ate one more and then there were three.
Oh! That monkey, with nothing to do
Ate one more and then there were two.
Oh! That monkey, playing in the sun
Ate one more and then there was one.
That little monkey, just for fun
Ate the last one then there was none.

Arooj Sohail Chaudhary (7)
Fairchildes Primary School, New Addington

Ginger The Hamster

I have a hamster girl, I call her Ginger.
She's furry, gingery with black eyes.
So sweet, so cute with chubby cheeks
When they're full of nuts and fruits.
She happily lives in her cage
Where she has her own playground.
Ginger loves to run all over it,
On the treadmill, on the slide,
On the swing, she plays all night.
She is part of our family.
I love my hamster.

Julia Gorka (6)
Fairchildes Primary School, New Addington

Hop And Stop

The first little rabbit went *hop, hop, hop*.
I said to the first rabbit, "Stop, stop, stop!"
The second little rabbit went run, run, run.
I said to the second rabbit, "Fun, fun, fun!"
The third little rabbit when *thump, thump, thump*.
I said to the third rabbit, "Jump, jump, jump!"
The fourth little rabbit went bye-bye.

Soliana Bekele (7)
Fairchildes Primary School, New Addington

Jake The Snake And Me

Once upon a time there was a snake
Called Jake and his life was fake
But all he did was give me a headache
So the only way I could make
Him be quiet was to push him into the lake
After he climbed out of the lake
I gave him a big fat cake
But the next day he was acting like a fool
So I told him that he was not cool
So he needed to go to school.

Farren Pickering (7)
Fairchildes Primary School, New Addington

Dancing Penguin

A brilliant dancer, an amazing talker,
A nimble ninja, a nosy head,
A flipper and a tripper,
A laugher and a lover,
Someone 1.7 metres,
Who eats anchovy pizza,
Lives in a ten-floor mansion,
But when he's not dancing
He's painting amazing pictures
Of his favourite band called the Migrators,
He loves making dance moves.

Levi Amoah (8)
Fairchildes Primary School, New Addington

Tom Cat

Here comes Tom the cat,
Taking place on his mat,
Licking food off his paw,
Waiting for Tiggs from next door,
A bang on the fence,
Makes Tom jump with suspense,
He takes a look,
It's only Tiggs that made him shook,
Time to play some games,
Before it rains,
Playing with his friend,
Until the day ends.

Leo Lambeth (6)
Fairchildes Primary School, New Addington

The Snake Named Jake

Once upon a time
There was a snake named Jake.
Jake was a very nice snake
But one day he got very annoying
So I pushed Jake into the lake
Then he pushed me into the lake
So then I gave him a big, fat cake
So then I told him to save some for me
But he didn't save some for me.

Blen Berhe (7)
Fairchildes Primary School, New Addington

My Friend The Gruffalo

Do you know the Gruffalo?

He is big and scary but he has a big heart and is friendly.
He walks around the woods, looking for yummy food.
He looks like a monster but he is soft like a teddy bear.

This is the Gruffalo.
My friend the Gruffalo.

Jeremiah Amoah (7)
Fairchildes Primary School, New Addington

My Pet Dog

My pet dog is small, friendly and clever,
Her favourite game is tugging at leather.

She makes me happy when I am sad,
She comforts me when I am mad.

She loves lots of cuddles
And jumping in muddy puddles.

Marios Jones (7)
Fairchildes Primary School, New Addington

Little Rabbit

I had a little rabbit
Whose name was Little Ben
I had a little rabbit
That would hop around all day
I had a little rabbit
That ate carrots from the garden
I had a little rabbit
That would snuggle up at night.

Liliana Cerullo (6)
Fairchildes Primary School, New Addington

Hop Hop Bunny

Fluffy bunny,
Friendly bunny,
Through the field she hops,
Through the day,
Through the night she never stops,
And at the end she says,
"Save me some carrot for another day,
So I can hop again."

Mia Baraniak (7)
Fairchildes Primary School, New Addington

Little Rabbit

Hop hop little rabbit
Hop hop, don't stop
Hop until you drop
But don't stop
Because you're my little rabbit
Your little hop will get you there
Don't hop too fast
Or else you will flop.

Mercedes Adesanya
Fairchildes Primary School, New Addington

Silly Old Cow

Silly old cow never listens
She is naughty and has no brain,
She lives in a barn next to a field of lambs.

Silly old cow makes silly jokes but laughs about them on her own.
Will silly old cow ever learn?

Josiah Amoah (7)
Fairchildes Primary School, New Addington

The Non-Hairy Scary Lion King

Once upon a day,
A hairy scary lion
Crossed a hairdresser's way.
He went to get his hair cut off,
With a huff and a puff.
Now he does not look scary anymore,
He looks friendly, just like before.

Faye Ogbuehi (6)
Fairchildes Primary School, New Addington

Snappe

The only way to make him quiet
Was to put him in a lake.
I made him tidy up.
Then he didn't know what two plus two was.
I said, "You need to go to school."

Leo Frost (7)
Fairchildes Primary School, New Addington

Life As A Lion

Fluffy hair,
He looks like a big cuddly teddy bear.
But with his sharp teeth,
He roams the Sahara desert,
Or maybe the jungle,
Looking for something to eat.
His roar is very loud
But he has to be quiet,
"*Shhh*," he can't make a sound.
It's a very scary sight,
As he pounces with all his might
On his meal that's in sight.
Tummy all nice and full,
It's time to relax now.
It's his favourite time of all,
Oh, how he loves being a lion.

Ariah Blue Griffiths-Proc (5)
Hadrian Primary School, South Shields

Gina The Giraffe

There once was a giraffe called Gina
Who wanted to be a ballerina
She was tall and kind
And friendly mind
And longed to go to the arena.

Gina's mam was called Monica
They lived in the grasslands in Africa
They ate carrots and leaves
And liked to believe
They both starred in the film Madagascar.

Mam would stride and Gina would bend
A friendly ear they would always lend
From tall trees they would munch
Whilst hanging out with their bunch
Any new mates they would always befriend.

So this is the story of Gina
Who wanted to be a ballerina
She would sing and dance
In her tutu she'd prance
And dream of being in the arena.

Emily Scott (5)
Hadrian Primary School, South Shields

The Early Morning Reindeer

Once I saw a reindeer,
Early Christmas Day,
When I took a closer look
It was eating hay.
The deer had large antlers
And lovely big brown eyes,
In amongst the forest
With all the butterflies.
What a beautiful Christmas morning
My family and I had,
After spotting Santa's reindeer
It made us all so glad.

Josie Willow Johnson (5)
Hadrian Primary School, South Shields

The Tiger

One day a stripy tiger called Lucy was being very scary.
All the animals wanted to run away.
The scared animal was called Mary.
Mary didn't like Lucy because she was loud.
In Asia Lucy liked eating other animals.
To catch the animals Lucy roared.
Mary tricked Lucy so she'd go.

Eva Hussain (5)
Hadrian Primary School, South Shields

Butterfly Song

The butterfly goes over the tree
The butterfly
It lands on the grass
It reminds me of a ladybird
Toto butterfly
The butterfly goes to get his friends
The butterfly hatches out of its egg
I love you
The butterfly is colourful
Pink and green and blue.

Arthur Deans Coffield (4)
Hadrian Primary School, South Shields

Hello Little Chicken

Hello little chicken
Eating seeds and grain
Let me in your tiny house
To see the eggs you've lain.

Good night little chicken
Sleep all snug and tight
Cockerel's song will wake me up
In the morning light.

Lily-Rose Gonzalez (5)
Hadrian Primary School, South Shields

It Is Long

It is covered in spots
Some could say they are dots
It is as tall as a tree
Five times as tall as me
It has hooves, ears and a tail
It's a giraffe, not a snail
And don't be silly
It's not for sale!

Rosa Mary (4)
Hadrian Primary School, South Shields

The Hunting Tiger

I have sharp teeth.
I am strong.
Roar!

I am orange and black.
Meat is my food!
I hunt, hunt, hunt.

Watch out!

Adam Elmenshawy
Hadrian Primary School, South Shields

The Penguin

I want to fly high up in the sky
And eat some pie but I can't
Because I am a penguin.

Rosie Cain (5)
Hadrian Primary School, South Shields

Whales

What a colossal, hard thing that's as hard as can be
And we don't have a clue why it sinks when it stops swimming.
Do you know whales need air to breathe?
What if it swims down?
Don't worry, they're just eating some krill and seaweed.
Blue whales live in all the oceans except the Arctic Ocean
Because it's so, so cold in the Arctic Ocean,
That's why there are no whales.
That was a really fun fact!

Rupert Crossdale (6)
Lawns Park Primary School, Leeds

The Terrific Tiger

The tiger who is terrific in size
Is stripy with sharp teeth and big, blue eyes.
He is orange and black,
Don't turn around or he will jump on your back!
He comes out at night
To give you a terrible fright.

Sophie Longley (6)
Lawns Park Primary School, Leeds

I Have A Lion

I have a lion
He is a big cat
He is fierce and hairy
But I don't mind that
He likes to eat meat
And likes to play in the grass
Chasing zebras
Having a blast.

Cecelia Manning (6)
Lawns Park Primary School, Leeds

The Sixteen-Legged Spider

Once upon a time lived a spider with sixteen legs and he was hanging his washing with pegs.
He had some trousers with sixteen legs and for breakfast he had some eggs.

Amber Ghatrora (5)
Lawns Park Primary School, Leeds

Funny Cat Poem

There once was an old tabby
Who was also very blabby
He told his friends he was a king
And a cat that could sing
But he was only a cabbie.

Elisha Hewson (6)
Lawns Park Primary School, Leeds

The Delicious Breakfast

D eep inside a wet and dark cave lives a monstrous creature
R oaring so loud the poor Earth trembles
A tasty full English breakfast fills him up for the day
G iant colourful dragon looks so friendly but is he?
O h no! Watch out!
N *ooo!* He opens his huge mouth and shows his sharp teeth.

Jenson Ainsworth (6)
Longshaw Infant School, Blackburn

The Bloodthirsty Dragon

D eadly dragons fill the street with fiery intimidation
R oars, knights gather around
A ngrily trying to save the pretty princess
G ood villagers need their friendly princess in a beautiful castle
O n a luscious green hill
N ever stop believing your dream can come true!

Lottie-Mae Egan (5)
Longshaw Infant School, Blackburn

The Not-So-Friendly Dragon

D eep, deep cave where there lives a monstrous creature
R ed dragons are flying in the dark sky
A n excited dragon is eating people
G etting more friends
O pening his mouth to show his sharp teeth
N oisy dotty dragons are flying, watch out!

Olivia Clarke (6)
Longshaw Infant School, Blackburn

Scary

D ark in a cave is a scary monster
R ed monster goes out of the deep cave
A ngry monster is stomping
G reat monster makes the earth shake by stomping
O nly the monster blows the roofs off the houses
N ow the monster flies back to the cave.

Caleb Bennett (5)
Longshaw Infant School, Blackburn

Dragon!

D eep inside the gloomy cave
R ed shiny eyes in the dark
A bove the fluffy clouds he flies
G igantic wings are flapping
O range fiery breath that is very hot
N o, don't go in there, you won't come out alive!

Habiba Zanid (6)
Longshaw Infant School, Blackburn

Dragon!

D eep in the dark gloomy cave
R ed spiky body
A bove the castle his wings are soaring in the storm
G igantic wings are flapping
O range fiery breath
N o, don't go in there, you won't come out alive!

Skylar Greenwood (6)
Longshaw Infant School, Blackburn

My Rainbow Dragon

D eep in a wet cave there lived a creature.
R ed fire breathing.
A long time ago there lived a dragon.
G lowing rainbow dragon with scaly skin.
O nly alone, wet scaly dragon.
N ow the scary dragon is mad.

Sydney Greenwood (6)
Longshaw Infant School, Blackburn

The Terrifying Dragon

D eadly fire-breathing dragons
R ampage through the streets
A colossal, bloodthirsty
G ruesome, ugly dragon has sharp teeth and
O ld claws
N ever go near the threatening dragon or it will eat your bones.

Draigh Gibbons (6)
Longshaw Infant School, Blackburn

Scary Dragon

D eep cave with scary bats.
R oaring hot flaming fire.
A mysterious creature flying in the sky.
G reen prickly scales are on his back.
O range cave is deep in the forest.
N ice dragon is here to play.

Alice Lianne Kenny (6)
Longshaw Infant School, Blackburn

My Dragon Swims!

D eep in a wet cave lived a ferocious evil creature
R ed hot, breathing fire in the sky
A nasty, mean creature is swimming
G oing to your pool
O range scales, it's a dragon
N ever need to shout.

Aurora-Rose Bentley (6)
Longshaw Infant School, Blackburn

Good Little Dragon

D eep in a lovely cave
"R oar!" the creature screams but is he scary?
A ctually he is kind and caring
G ood little dragon flying high in the sky
O h so cute!
N ow he will blow a love heart.

Azma Anwar (6)
Longshaw Infant School, Blackburn

Dragon

D eep in a dark cave
R ed beady gloomy eyes staring at me
A bove the clouds there are flapping wings
G igantic and dark then a rainbow
O range fire comes out of the cave
N oisy people are running.

Letty Riley (5)
Longshaw Infant School, Blackburn

The Beastly Dragon

D own in the deep deep cave there's a dirty dragon who
R oars with all its might.
A gigantic heavy tail and some
G ruesome pointy teeth.
O nly dare to go near if you are
N asty and brave.

Winter Daye (6)
Longshaw Infant School, Blackburn

Tasty Teachers

D iving into the sky
R unning down the road
A mysterious thing that eats smelly teachers
G ood boy, he eats no children
O pen my front door, he lives in my house
N ight night my blue dragon.

Baboucarr MP Van Eyndhoven (6)
Longshaw Infant School, Blackburn

Dragon!

D eep in the dark cave
R ed shining gloomy eyes in the dark
A bove the white clouds soaring
G igantic wings flapping
O range fiery breath
N o, don't go in there, you will never come back!

Alexis Williams (6)
Longshaw Infant School, Blackburn

The Mighty Dragon

D ancing in the deep dark cave there was a dragon called
R ice and he is colossal
A very ugly tail
G inormous wings are
O n this deadly beast
N ever go close to it or it will eat you all up!

Jonathan Zagara (5)
Longshaw Infant School, Blackburn

The Red-Eyed Dragon

D ark cave at night
R ed eyes glow
A ll of a sudden he eats my friend Eric
G iant wings to help him fly
O pen wide to see his big sharp teeth
N ow it is night-time, he goes back to his cave.

Bilal Majid (5)
Longshaw Infant School, Blackburn

Watch Out!

D eep in a black cave there was a scary creature
R ed fire on houses
A creature was breathing fire
G reat huge sharp teeth
O ut came his claws
N ow the creature goes to another village.

Lisa Lin (6)
Longshaw Infant School, Blackburn

Dragon

D eep in the gloomy cave
R ed shining eyes
A bove the dark cave he flies
G igantic flying wings
O range fiery breath
N o, don't go in there, you won't come back alive!

Ionie Clarke (6)
Longshaw Infant School, Blackburn

The Pretty Dragon Is Kind

D ragons are kind and magnificent.
R oaring with fun.
A round the green tall forest.
G etting into mischief.
O n a bright sunny day.
N ever be scared because he is amazing.

Khadija Hafeji (6)
Longshaw Infant School, Blackburn

Where Is My Dragon?

D eep in a dark cave lives a good creature
R ipping through the sea
A tiny creature
G reedy creature eats meat
O range creature has a cute tail
N ever to be seen again.

Siena Riley (5)
Longshaw Infant School, Blackburn

Dragon!

D eep red eyes glowing in the dark cave
R oaring out of his throat
A bove the high mountains he lives
G rowling in the night
O range scaly tummy
N oisy people screaming.

Reece Thompson (6)
Longshaw Infant School, Blackburn

Dragon!

D eep in the gloomy cave
R ed spiky body
A bove the huge castle he turns
G igantic wings
O range fiery breath
N o, don't go in there, you won't come out alive!

Eva Slater (6)
Longshaw Infant School, Blackburn

Scary Dragon

D eep dark mountain
R ed-breathing dragon
A dark cave is a scary cave
G reen dragon is scary
O range dragon is naughty
N asty dragon is going back to the mountain.

Luke McCardle (6)
Longshaw Infant School, Blackburn

My Dragon

D eep in a tall mountain.
R ed dragon is nice.
A nd friendly.
G reen scaly dragon breathing fire.
O range dragon eats meat.
N aughty dragon wakes everything up.

Lydia Eddleston (5)
Longshaw Infant School, Blackburn

Dragon!

D eep in the dark cave
R ed gloomy eyes
A bove the white clouds he flies
G igantic wings flapping
O range fiery breath
N oisy people screaming in fear.

Isabelle Hargreaves (6)
Longshaw Infant School, Blackburn

My Cute Pink Dragon

D eep in a warm cave
R ed hot flames
A cute little creature
G lorious red and pink-scaled skin
O range spiky horns
N ice tiny dragon loves a cuddle.

Esmé Newton (6)
Longshaw Infant School, Blackburn

My Dragon

D ragon
R oars at people when he is mad
A wful dragon with red eyes
G reat big wings
O nly eats scary people
N aughty dragon, do not touch him.

Riley Ferrari (6)
Longshaw Infant School, Blackburn

Dragon

D eep in the dark cave
R ed evil eyes
A bove the fluffy clouds it flies into the sky
G igantic wings
O range hot fire
N oisy people screaming.

Jack Harris (5)
Longshaw Infant School, Blackburn

The Nice Dragon

D own in the castle there is a
R eally little dragon
A nd he lives happily
G oing on a green hill
O ther dragons love him
N ow he is adorable.

Daisy Wickham (5)
Longshaw Infant School, Blackburn

Dragon!

D eep in a dark cave
R ed eyes glowing
A bove in the sky flying
G igantic body
O range and red fire
N o way you will survive!

Ellis Shaw (5)
Longshaw Infant School, Blackburn

Dragons

D angerous and colossal
R eally bad at flying
A ngry and scary
G reedy and eat fish
O pen red eyes
N asty and bloodthirsty.

Nicolle Ndlovu (6)
Longshaw Infant School, Blackburn

Dragon

D elicate and dainty
R elaxed and lovely
A nxious and adorable
G entle and great
O penhearted
N ice and caring.

Lily Greenhough (6)
Longshaw Infant School, Blackburn

Dragons

D ancing dragon is cute
R eally shy
A nxious
G ood and gorgeous
O pen cute eyes
N ice and hot pizza.

Austen Snape (6)
Longshaw Infant School, Blackburn

Dragons

D ainty and cute
R eally shy
A n apple eater
G reat at singing
O penhearted
N ice and gentle.

Tiffany Abram (6)
Longshaw Infant School, Blackburn

Dragon

D angerous
R eally angry
A bloodthirsty creature
G rown-up eater
O pen-wide mouth
N asty.

Alyssa Fitzpatrick (6)
Longshaw Infant School, Blackburn

Dragons

D ainty and cute
R eally shy
A nxious and kind
G reat saver
O penhearted
N ice at flying.

Issac Cocker (6)
Longshaw Infant School, Blackburn

The Cute Dragon

D eadly beastly dragons are evil and angry
R oarsome
A ngry
G reedy
O nes are
N asty.

Scarlett Jackson (5)
Longshaw Infant School, Blackburn

Dragon

D angerous
R ed fire breathing
A nxious and cute
G orgeous
O pen eyes
N ice.

Abigail Zalewska (5)
Longshaw Infant School, Blackburn

Dragon

D angerous
R eally terrifying
A ngry
G reedy
O range breathing
N asty.

Alfie-James McGlinn (5)
Longshaw Infant School, Blackburn

Roar

R ed dangerous eyes.
O range boiling fire.
A ngry evil dragon.
R ushing through the sky.

Hunter Jackson (6)
Longshaw Infant School, Blackburn

My Dragon

D ark cave
R *ar!*
A loud
G reedy
O ld
N aughty dragon.

Seth Nyarambi (6)
Longshaw Infant School, Blackburn

Roar!

R ed dangerous eyes
O range mighty fire
A ngry loud roar!
R ushing through the sky.

Aibhlinn Griffiths (6)
Longshaw Infant School, Blackburn

Dragon

D ancing dragon
R ed tail
A ngry
G orgeous
O pen eyes
N ice.

Eli Martindale (5)
Longshaw Infant School, Blackburn

Dragon

D angerous
R eally toxic
A nxious
G reedy
O pen eyes
N ice.

Luca Popa (5)
Longshaw Infant School, Blackburn

Dangerous

D eadly
R eally evil
A ngry
G reedy
O range and cute
N ice.

Sophia-Lillie Cantwell (5)
Longshaw Infant School, Blackburn

Roar

R ed evil dragon
O range hot fire
A ngry scary wings
R ushing through the sky.

Caoimhe Hamill (5)
Longshaw Infant School, Blackburn

Dragon

D angerous
R ed hot
A ngry
G reedy
O range tail
N asty.

Aubrey Hosker (5)
Longshaw Infant School, Blackburn

Roar

R ed scaly body
O range hot fire
A ngry evil dragon
R oaring loud.

Shay Ruddy (6)
Longshaw Infant School, Blackburn

Roar

R ed scary eyes
O range hot fire
A ngry dragon
R oaring loud.

Maira Bisharet (6)
Longshaw Infant School, Blackburn

Lions

Lions smell of zebras because they want to hunt them down to death.
Lions look scary so they can scare people because they have glowing orange eyes.
Lions sound like a beast roaring so they can scare people and chase them to death.
Lions feel smooth, soft and fluffy on their skin so they can keep their skin warm.
Lions taste of raw meat.

Amelia-Rose Lings (7)
St John's CofE Primary School, Stapleford

Lions

Lions smell the blood of a zebra drifting through the savannah.
Lions look terrifying because they have big manes and have orange eyes like the sun!
Lions sound like a T-rex so they can scare their prey.
Lions feel like a rough rock glistening in the sun.
Lions taste like crunchy meat, really juicy and fat.

Lydia Mathison (7)
St John's CofE Primary School, Stapleford

Lions

Lions smell of zebras and lions smell of meat because they have meat in their bodies.
Lions look terrifying because they have sharp teeth.
Lions sound like a big dinosaur so that they can show who is the boss.
Lions feel bumpy, soft, rough and furry.
Lions taste like hairy and disgusting creatures.

Hanna Bella Herczeg (7)
St John's CofE Primary School, Stapleford

Lions

Lions smell the blood of zebras because they have a great sense of smell.
Lions look terrifying so that they can scare other animals and enemies.
Lions like a roar of terror so they can show who is boss.
Lions feel rough and soft and fluffy and hard.
Lions taste of disgusting, hairy, horrible meat!

Merry Lyons (7)
St John's CofE Primary School, Stapleford

Lions

Lions smell the zebras in the grass.
Lions look terrifying because they eat animals.
Lions sound like a roaring T-rex about to eat a zebra.
Lions feel like soft fur.
Lions taste of tough, hard, juicy meat.

Clover (7)
St John's CofE Primary School, Stapleford

Lions

Lions smell like prey's blood and zebra.
Lions sound like a roaring T-rex.
Lions taste like bloody meat.
Lions look like they are about to eat me.
Lions feel like a cuddly teddy bear.

Zuriella (7)
St John's CofE Primary School, Stapleford

Lions

Lions smell of animals like zebras.
Lions look terrifying with bloody teeth.
Lions sound terrifying so they are not kind!
Lions feel soft and cuddly.
Lions taste like brown squishy meat.

Beth Tan (5)
St John's CofE Primary School, Stapleford

Lions

Lions smell of the gleaming hot sun from above.
Lions look blood-covered because they want to fight.
Lions sound like fierce predators.
Lions feel fluffy.
Lions taste of hot dogs.

Ronnie Kirkpatrick (7)
St John's CofE Primary School, Stapleford

Lions

Lions smell of zebra.
Lions look fierce because they have sharp teeth.
Lions sound like roaring dinosaurs.
Lions feel like a furry cushion.
Lions taste of juicy orange meat.

Abraham Burton (6)
St John's CofE Primary School, Stapleford

Lions

Lions smell of zebras.
Lions look terrifying because they have big teeth.
Lions sound like dinosaurs.
Lions feel smooth like a rock.
Lions taste of juicy meat.

Jessica Mann (6)
St John's CofE Primary School, Stapleford

Lions

Lions smell of the hot sun.
Lions look scary when they open their mouth.
Lions feel soft.
Lions can hear enemies creeping upon them.
Lions taste like meat.

Nico O'Connor (7)
St John's CofE Primary School, Stapleford

Lions

Lions eat meat because they do.
Lions have big sharp teeth because they are shiny.
Lions sound like roaring.
Lions feel smooth.
Lions taste of meat.

Liliya White (6)
St John's CofE Primary School, Stapleford

Lions

Lions smell of meat.
Lions look terrifying. They have sharp teeth.
Lions sound like a dinosaur.
Lions feel soft.
Lions taste of meat.

Callum Allaway (6)
St John's CofE Primary School, Stapleford

Lions

Lions smell like meat.
Lions look scary.
Lions sound like a roaring T-rex.
Lions feel like a teddy bear.
Lions taste of berries.

Cyrus Bennett (6)
St John's CofE Primary School, Stapleford

Lions

Lions smell of tasty zebras.
Lions look fierce and scary.
Lions sound like loud roars.
Lions feel soft.
Lions taste like meat.

Harry McLaughlin (5)
St John's CofE Primary School, Stapleford

Lions

Lions smell of zebras.
Lions look scary.
Lions sound like, "*Roar!*"
Lions feel fluffy.
Lions taste of meat.

Ben White (6)
St John's CofE Primary School, Stapleford

Lions

Lions smell of animals.
Lions look brave and gold.
Lions sound like roaring enemies.
Lions feel soft.

Hollie Hutchinson (6)
St John's CofE Primary School, Stapleford

Lions

Lions smell of grass.
Lions look scary.
Lions roar.
Lions feel soft.
Lions taste of meat.

George (5), Frankie, Harry, Shelby & Hollie (6)
St John's CofE Primary School, Stapleford

Lions

Lions smell of grass.
Lions look scary.
Lions roar.
Lions feel soft.
Lions taste of meat.

Shelby Dackiw (6)
St John's CofE Primary School, Stapleford

Lions

Lions smell of grass.
Lions look scary.
Lions roar.
Lions feel soft.
Lions taste of meat.

Coleson-Christopher Lings (6)
St John's CofE Primary School, Stapleford

Lions

Lions smell of grass.
Lions roar like a T-rex.
Lions feel soft.
Lions taste of meat.

Anaya Gajendran (6)
St John's CofE Primary School, Stapleford

The White Stripy Tiger

The tiger can see all the long grass
The long trees and the rain.
She can hear the long, wavy trees
The grass and the people walking and talking.
She can feel the floor, the rocks
And the long grass with her lovely paws.
The tiger can taste the delicious meat in her mouth.
She can smell the meat and the people passing by.

Ella Uzor (7)
St Maria Goretti Primary School, Cranhill

The Big Sea Lion

The sea lion sees the clear water.
She smells fish swimming around her.
She tastes the salty water.
The sea lion hears the water splashing in her ears.
The sea lion can feel the slimy seaweed going on her body.

Aveen Mussa (7)
St Maria Goretti Primary School, Cranhill

The Black Sea Lion

The black sea lion tastes salty water and it tastes good.
He smells the muddy rocks with slimy seaweed.
He feels stinky sand with dirty grass.
He sees giant buildings crashing.
He hears kids shouting.

Umar Eskiev (7)
St Maria Goretti Primary School, Cranhill

The Tiger

The tiger hears a block of sheep in the distance.
It smells the meat of the sheep.
He feels the ground and the grass.
He sees the sheep, now it's got the sheep
And now it tastes the meat.

Cooper Muir (7)
St Maria Goretti Primary School, Cranhill

Smart Sea Lion

The sea lion hears a ton of fish swimming and waves.
He tastes fish, meat and seabirds.
He sees crabs scuttling and birds flying.
The sea lion smells slimy seaweed and people.

Osewe Inyinbor (7)
St Maria Goretti Primary School, Cranhill

The Tiger

The tiger smells trees
And green, wavy grass,
She hears people,
She tastes green grass,
The tiger sees the grass,
She feels mud on her paws.

Isla Clark (7)
St Maria Goretti Primary School, Cranhill

About The Lion

The lion hears the people walking
She feels the rocks on the ground
She smells the people eating tasty sandwiches
She touches her paw on the people.

Orlaith Walsh (7)
St Maria Goretti Primary School, Cranhill

The Lion

The lion sees prey and it's running.
He feels the waving grass.
He smells his breath.
The lion hears people talking
And tastes tasty food.

Ray Campbell (7)
St Maria Goretti Primary School, Cranhill

All Dolphins

Dolphins, oh dolphins
I'll ride on your back
But maybe, oh maybe
I'll never come back
I'll ride on your back
Your slippery wet back
We'll go to the ocean
And never come back.

Dolphins, oh dolphins
We'll swim and have fun
We'll play all day
In the glistening sun
At night-time we'll sleep
Under the bright shining moon
And the waves of the ocean
Will sing us a tune.

Aoife Maguire (7)
St Mary's Primary School, Bellanaleck

My Poem About Dogs

Dogs, dogs, so tiny and small
Can you see them in the house at all?
Dogs are cuddly
Dogs are cute and intelligent animals
They are smart and they chase after you
I wish I could be one
Too bad I am not!
I love them so much
And I love taking him out for walks
And when he runs his ears flop
It is so cute!
And sometimes he does very cool tricks!
And again, I just need to say
He is so cute!

Aoife McArdle (7)
St Mary's Primary School, Bellanaleck

The Flamingo

Oh flamingo, oh flamingo
Very pink
Very, very big animal
Very funny and cool
I see them at the zoo
They stand on one leg
They turn their head upside down to eat
I love them *so* much
I wish I could be one
Too bad I am not
I love flamingos
Maybe you do too.

Ella McCusker (7)
St Mary's Primary School, Bellanaleck

Monkeys!

Monkeys, monkeys are so silly,
They make me laugh every day.
Eating bananas all the time,
I'm trying to make this poem rhyme.
Monkeys like to swing up high,
In the treetops touching the sky.
Monkeys, monkeys swing from tree to tree,
How you like to be free!

Sianna McGahey (7)
St Mary's Primary School, Bellanaleck

Cheeky Monkey!

Monkey, monkey, so tiny and small
Will you be my friend at all?
You swing from branches and you jump around
I look for you but you can't be found!
Come and play, funny monkey!
Let's eat bananas, dance and swing
We can do anything.

Aibreán Rooney (7)
St Mary's Primary School, Bellanaleck

The Rare Red Pandas

Red panda, red panda,
So rare and so small.
Can I find you in a zoo at all?
I think I can find you on a mountain so tall.
I just want to find you so we can be friends.
Can we, red panda?
Please, you are such a beautiful animal.

Maria Kelly (7)
St Mary's Primary School, Bellanaleck

Koala At The Zoo

Koala, koala, I saw one at the zoo
I love koalas and I love you.
Koala, koala, so cute and small
Can you see them in the Eucalyptus tree?

Kíla Gallagher (7)
St Mary's Primary School, Bellanaleck

The King Of The Pandas

The king is black and white
It normally doesn't hunt in the night
It just hunts in the light
Yes, it hunts in the light.

Charlie Bannon (7)
St Mary's Primary School, Bellanaleck

Owls In The Night

Owl, owl, kakoo, kakoo
I hear a noise, is that you?
I think I see you in a tree
Kakoo, kakoo
Do you see me?

Anna Kelly (7)
St Mary's Primary School, Bellanaleck

The Black Cheetah

Cheetahs, cheetahs
Cheetahs are fast
Cheetahs, cheetahs
Cheetahs are black and stripy!

Shane Maguire-Reilly (7)
St Mary's Primary School, Bellanaleck

YOUNG WRITERS INFORMATION

We hope you have enjoyed reading this book – and that you will continue to in the coming years.

If you're the parent or family member of an enthusiastic poet or story writer, do visit our website **www.youngwriters.co.uk/subscribe** and sign up to receive news, competitions, writing challenges and tips, activities and much, much more! There's lots to keep budding writers motivated!

If you would like to order further copies of this book, or any of our other titles, then please give us a call or order via your online account.

Young Writers
Remus House
Coltsfoot Drive
Peterborough
PE2 9BF
(01733) 890066
info@youngwriters.co.uk

Join in the conversation!
Tips, news, giveaways and much more!

YoungWritersUK   YoungWritersCW   youngwriterscw

SCAN ME TO WATCH THE POETRY SAFARI VIDEO!